Write Your Vision - Habakkuk 2:2

Write Your Vision - Habakkuk 2:2

Write Your Vision - Habakkuk 2:2

Write Your Vision - Habakkuk 2:2

Write Your Vision - Habakkuk 2:2

Write Your Vision - Habakkuk 2:2

Write Your Vision - Habakkuk 2:2

Write Your Vision - Habakkuk 2:2

Write Your Vision - Habakkuk 2:2

Write Your Vision - Habakkuk 2:2

Write Your Vision - Habakkuk 2:2

Write Your Vision - Habakkuk 2:2

Write Your Vision - Habakkuk 2:2

Write Your Vision - Habakkuk 2:2

Write Your Vision - Habakkuk 2:2

Write Your Vision - Habakkuk 2:2

Write Your Vision - Habakkuk 2:2

Write Your Vision - Habakkuk 2:2

Write Your Vision - Habakkuk 2:2

Write Your Vision - Habakkuk 2:2

Write Your Vision - Habakkuk 2:2

Write Your Vision - Habakkuk 2:2

Write Your Vision - Habakkuk 2:2

1

Write Your Vision - Habakkuk 2:2

Write Your Vision - Habakkuk 2:2

Write Your Vision – Habakkuk 2:2

Write Your Vision - Habakkuk 2:2

Write Your Vision - Habakkuk 2:2

Write Your Vision - Habakkuk 2:2

Write Your Vision - Habakkuk 2:2

Write Your Vision - Habakkuk 2:2

Write Your Vision - Habakkuk 2:2

Write Your Vision - Habakkuk 2:2

Write Your Vision - Habakkuk 2:2

Write Your Vision - Habakkuk 2:2

Write Your Vision - Habakkuk 2:2

Write Your Vision - Habakkuk 2:2

_____
_____
_____
_____
_____
_____
_____
_____
_____
_____
_____
_____
_____
_____
_____
_____
_____
_____
_____
_____
_____
_____
_____
_____
_____
_____
_____
_____
_____
_____
_____

Write Your Vision - Habakkuk 2:2

Write Your Vision - Habakkuk 2:2

Write Your Vision - Habakkuk 2:2

Write Your Vision - Habakkuk 2:2

Write Your Vision - Habakkuk 2:2

Write Your Vision - Habakkuk 2:2

Write Your Vision - Habakkuk 2:2

Write Your Vision - Habakkuk 2:2

_____

_____

_____

_____

_____

_____

_____

_____

_____

_____

_____

_____

_____

_____

_____

_____

_____

_____

_____

_____

_____

_____

_____

_____

_____

_____

_____

_____

Write Your Vision - Habakkuk 2:2

Write Your Vision - Habakkuk 2:2

Write Your Vision - Habakkuk 2:2

Write Your Vision - Habakkuk 2:2

Write Your Vision - Habakkuk 2:2

Write Your Vision - Habakkuk 2:2

Write Your Vision - Habakkuk 2:2

Write Your Vision - Habakkuk 2:2

Write Your Vision - Habakkuk 2:2

Write Your Vision – Habakkuk 2:2

Write Your Vision - Habakkuk 2:2

_____

_____

_____

_____

_____

_____

_____

_____

_____

_____

_____

_____

_____

_____

_____

_____

_____

_____

_____

_____

_____

_____

_____

_____

_____

_____

_____

_____

_____

_____

Write Your Vision - Habakkuk 2:2

Write Your Vision - Habakkuk 2:2

Write Your Vision - Habakkuk 2:2

Write Your Vision - Habakkuk 2:2

Write Your Vision - Habakkuk 2:2

Write Your Vision - Habakkuk 2:2

Write Your Vision - Habakkuk 2:2

Write Your Vision - Habakkuk 2:2

Write Your Vision - Habakkuk 2:2

Write Your Vision - Habakkuk 2:2

Write Your Vision - Habakkuk 2:2

_____
_____
_____
_____
_____
_____
_____
_____
_____
_____
_____
_____
_____
_____
_____
_____
_____
_____
_____
_____
_____
_____
_____
_____
_____
_____
_____
_____
_____
_____
_____
_____

Write Your Vision - Habakkuk 2:2

Write Your Vision - Habakkuk 2:2

Write Your Vision - Habakkuk 2:2

Write Your Vision - Habakkuk 2:2

Write Your Vision - Habakkuk 2:2

Write Your Vision - Habakkuk 2:2

Write Your Vision - Habakkuk 2:2

Write Your Vision - Habakkuk 2:2

Write Your Vision - Habakkuk 2:2

Write Your Vision - Habakkuk 2:2

Write Your Vision - Habakkuk 2:2

Write Your Vision - Habakkuk 2:2

Write Your Vision - Habakkuk 2:2

Write Your Vision - Habakkuk 2:2

Write Your Vision - Habakkuk 2:2

Write Your Vision - Habakkuk 2:2

Write Your Vision - Habakkuk 2:2

Write Your Vision - Habakkuk 2:2

Write Your Vision - Habakkuk 2:2

Write Your Vision - Habakkuk 2:2

Write Your Vision - Habakkuk 2:2

Write Your Vision - Habakkuk 2:2

Write Your Vision - Habakkuk 2:2

Write Your Vision - Habakkuk 2:2

_____
_____
_____
_____
_____
_____
_____
_____
_____
_____
_____
_____
_____
_____
_____
_____
_____
_____
_____
_____
_____
_____
_____
_____
_____
_____
_____
_____
_____
_____

Write Your Vision - Habakkuk 2:2

_____
_____
_____
_____
_____
_____
_____
_____
_____
_____
_____
_____
_____
_____
_____
_____
_____
_____
_____
_____
_____
_____
_____
_____
_____
_____
_____
_____
_____

Write Your Vision - Habakkuk 2:2

Write Your Vision - Habakkuk 2:2

Write Your Vision - Habakkuk 2:2

Write Your Vision - Habakkuk 2:2

Write Your Vision - Habakkuk 2:2

Write Your Vision - Habakkuk 2:2

Write Your Vision - Habakkuk 2:2

Write Your Vision – Habakkuk 2:2

Write Your Vision - Habakkuk 2:2

Write Your Vision - Habakkuk 2:2

Write Your Vision - Habakkuk 2:2

Write Your Vision - Habakkuk 2:2

Write Your Vision – Habakkuk 2:2

Write Your Vision - Habakkuk 2:2

Write Your Vision - Habakkuk 2:2

Write Your Vision - Habakkuk 2:2

Write Your Vision - Habakkuk 2:2

Write Your Vision - Habakkuk 2:2

Write Your Vision - Habakkuk 2:2

Write Your Vision - Habakkuk 2:2

Write Your Vision - Habakkuk 2:2

Write Your Vision - Habakkuk 2:2

Write Your Vision – Habakkuk 2:2

Write Your Vision - Habakkuk 2:2

Write Your Vision - Habakkuk 2:2

Write Your Vision - Habakkuk 2:2

Write Your Vision - Habakkuk 2:2

Write Your Vision - Habakkuk 2:2

Write Your Vision - Habakkuk 2:2

Write Your Vision - Habakkuk 2:2

_____

_____

_____

_____

_____

_____

_____

_____

_____

_____

_____

_____

_____

_____

_____

_____

_____

_____

_____

_____

_____

_____

_____

_____

_____

_____

_____

_____

_____

_____

_____

_____

_____

_____

_____

Write Your Vision - Habakkuk 2:2

Write Your Vision - Habakkuk 2:2

Write Your Vision - Habakkuk 2:2

Write Your Vision - Habakkuk 2:2

_____
_____
_____
_____
_____
_____
_____
_____
_____
_____
_____
_____
_____
_____
_____
_____
_____
_____
_____
_____
_____
_____
_____
_____
_____
_____
_____
_____
_____
_____

Write Your Vision - Habakkuk 2:2

_____
_____
_____
_____
_____
_____
_____
_____
_____
_____
_____
_____
_____
_____
_____
_____
_____
_____
_____
_____
_____
_____
_____
_____
_____
_____
_____
_____
_____

_____
_____
_____
_____
_____
_____
_____
_____
_____
_____
_____
_____
_____
_____
_____
_____
_____
_____
_____
_____
_____
_____
_____
_____
_____
_____
_____
_____

Write Your Vision - Habakkuk 2:2

_____
_____
_____
_____
_____
_____
_____
_____
_____
_____
_____
_____
_____
_____
_____
_____
_____
_____
_____
_____
_____
_____
_____
_____
_____
_____
_____
_____
_____
_____
_____
_____

Write Your Vision – Habakkuk 2:2

Write Your Vision - Habakkuk 2:2

Write Your Vision - Habakkuk 2:2

Write Your Vision - Habakkuk 2:2

Write Your Vision - Habakkuk 2:2

Write Your Vision - Habakkuk 2:2

Write Your Vision - Habakkuk 2:2

Write Your Vision - Habakkuk 2:2

_____
_____
_____
_____
_____
_____
_____
_____
_____
_____
_____
_____
_____
_____
_____
_____
_____
_____
_____
_____
_____
_____
_____
_____
_____
_____
_____
_____
_____
_____
_____
_____

Write Your Vision - Habakkuk 2:2

Write Your Vision - Habakkuk 2:2

Write Your Vision - Habakkuk 2:2

Write Your Vision - Habakkuk 2:2

Write Your Vision - Habakkuk 2:2

Write Your Vision - Habakkuk 2:2

Write Your Vision - Habakkuk 2:2

Write Your Vision - Habakkuk 2:2

Write Your Vision - Habakkuk 2:2

Write Your Vision - Habakkuk 2:2

Write Your Vision - Habakkuk 2:2

Write Your Vision - Habakkuk 2:2

Write Your Vision - Habakkuk 2:2

Write Your Vision - Habakkuk 2:2

Write Your Vision - Habakkuk 2:2

Write Your Vision - Habakkuk 2:2

Write Your Vision - Habakkuk 2:2

_____
_____
_____
_____
_____
_____
_____
_____
_____
_____
_____
_____
_____
_____
_____
_____
_____
_____
_____
_____
_____
_____
_____
_____
_____
_____
_____
_____
_____
_____

Write Your Vision - Habakkuk 2:2

Write Your Vision - Habakkuk 2:2

Write Your Vision - Habakkuk 2:2

Write Your Vision - Habakkuk 2:2

Write Your Vision - Habakkuk 2:2

Write Your Vision - Habakkuk 2:2

Write Your Vision - Habakkuk 2:2

Write Your Vision - Habakkuk 2:2

Write Your Vision – Habakkuk 2:2

Write Your Vision - Habakkuk 2:2

Write Your Vision - Habakkuk 2:2

Write Your Vision - Habakkuk 2:2

Write Your Vision - Habakkuk 2:2

Your Story Matters
Order Insert HAB22 at
www.taylormadepublishingfl.com
TMPFLORIDA Publication
ISBN 978-1-953526-18-2

Write Your Vision - Habakkuk 2:2